* * * * *

'*The Autistic Teen Girl's School Survival Guide* is fantastic – easy to read, clear and relatable. It's packed full of tips that are easy to implement; a real go-to guide.'

– Sarah Wild, headteacher of
Limpsfield Grange School, Surrey

* * * * *

'As I was reading this all I could visualize was a beautiful autistic gemstone that my brain had invented; and that gemstone is called Gracie Barlow. This books shines – just like Gracie's personality – and is so full of wisdom and, excuse the pun, grace that it should be compulsory reading for anyone who has the remotest interest in creating safe and positive spaces for autistic young people.'

– Dr Luke Beardon, Senior Lecturer in
Autism at Sheffield Hallam University

* * * * *

T0299615

of related interest

The Spectrum Girl's Survival Guide
How to Grow Up Awesome and Autistic
Siena Castellon
Foreword by Temple Grandin
ISBN 978 1 78775 183 5
eISBN 978 1 80501 517 8

The Awesome Autistic Go-To Guide
A Practical Handbook for Autistic Teens and Tweens
Yenn Purkis and Tanya Masterman
Foreword by Emma Goodall
ISBN 978 1 78775 316 7
eISBN 978 1 78775 317 4

The Awesome Autistic Guide to Other Humans
Relationships with Friends and Family
Yenn Purkis and Tanya Masterman
ISBN 978 1 83997 740 4
eISBN 978 1 83997 741 1
Awesome Guides for Amazing Autistic Kids

The Awesome Autistic Guide to Being Proud
Feeling Good About Who You Are
Yenn Purkis and Tanya Masterman
ISBN 978 1 83997 736 7
eISBN 978 1 83997 737 4
Awesome Guides for Amazing Autistic Kids

The Awesome Autistic Guide to Feelings and Emotions
Finding Your Comfort Zone
Yenn Purkis and Tanya Masterman
ISBN 978 1 83997 738 1
eISBN 978 1 83997 739 8
Awesome Guides for Amazing Autistic Kids

THE
AUTISTIC TEEN
GIRL'S SCHOOL
SURVIVAL GUIDE

Gracie Barlow

Jessica Kingsley Publishers
London and Philadelphia

First published in Great Britain in 2025 by Jessica Kingsley Publishers
An imprint of John Murray Press

2

Copyright © Gracie Barlow 2025

Content Warning: This book contains mentions of self-harm, drug and alcohol abuse, and disordered eating.

A CIP catalogue record for this title is available from
the British Library and the Library of Congress

ISBN 978 1 80501 234 4
eISBN 978 1 80501 235 1

Printed and bound in Great Britain by Clays Ltd

Jessica Kingsley Publishers' policy is to use papers that
are natural, renewable and recyclable products and made
from wood grown in sustainable forests. The logging and
manufacturing processes are expected to conform to the
environmental regulations of the country of origin.

Jessica Kingsley Publishers
Carmelite House
50 Victoria Embankment
London EC4Y 0DZ

www.jkp.com

John Murray Press
Part of Hodder & Stoughton Ltd
An Hachette Company

The authorised representative in the EEA is Hachette Ireland,
8 Castlecourt Centre, Dublin 15, D15 XTP3, Ireland (email: info@hbgi.ie)

Contents

Acknowledgements

The book you're holding exists because of my experiences as an autistic girl in mainstream secondary school. My passage from year 7 to year 13 was eventful, emotional, exhilarating and excruciating.

There are certain school staff who deserve special mention for strapping in beside me on this rollercoaster of a ride: Ali B for cheering me on during challenging times, Aniff for fuelling my dramatic fervour and bringing me back from Broadway alive, Emma B for tea, biscuits and a total acceptance of my potty mouth, and Ms Mapp for talking my anxiety down and my academic confidence up.

And Mel G. There aren't enough words to describe how

grateful I am to you (cringe!). You have **never** given up on me, even when I 'sacked' you.

To mental health practitioners Julie and Trudie, you have both played key roles in my emotional well-being. I wouldn't be here without you.

My heartfelt thanks to the amazing experts who have racked their brilliant brains providing top advice over the following pages: Dr Luke Beardon, author of *Autism and Asperger Syndrome in Children* and Senior Lecturer at Sheffield Hallam University's Autism Centre; Siena Castellon, autism advocate and author of *The Spectrum Girl's Survival Guide*; and Mair Elliott, young patient activist and author of *From Hurt to Hope: Stories of Mental Health, Mental Illness, and Being Autistic.*

Also, Jo Egerton, schools research consultant and co-editor of *Girls and Autism*; Francesca Happé, Professor of Cognitive Neuroscience, King's College London, and co-editor of *Girls and Autism*; and Georgia Harper, autistic campaigner and Policy and Public Affairs Officer for national research charity Autistica.

Finally, Victoria Honeybourne, specialist advisory

teacher and author of *Educating and Supporting Autistic Girls*; Alis Rowe, autistic entrepreneur, scriptwriter and film director, and author of *The Girl with the Curly Hair: Asperger's and Me*; and Sarah Wild, headteacher of Limpsfield Grange School for girls with communication and interaction difficulties.

Thanks also to Helen Evans, CEO for Cavernoma Alliance UK, who, having read my book, insisted I should publish, and Amy Lankester-Owen, Editorial Director at Jessica Kingsley Publishers, who made this a reality.

And then, to my friends and family, human and canine. Doug, you weren't officially a therapy dog, but you unconditionally comforted me through some properly rubbish times. Margot isn't physically big enough to fill your space, but she's trying!

Hanna, I never believed I was worthy of a friendship like ours. You are a phenomenal human and have made my life better. Todd, 'sincerity is scary', but you are my other half, my safe place.

To Nana. You never got to see this book in print, but your eternal wisdom benefits me, daily. My 'little' brother Willem, decent, patient, captivatingly neurodiverse and the master of 'cheer-me-up' memes. Thanks, Dad, for your proofreading, taxi driving and lighting the touch paper on my vinyl obsession.

And finally, to my magnificent Mum, a mighty rock and the most awesome advocate any autistic girl could wish to have. If I did hugging, you'd be first in line. ♥

Introduction

Okay, so where do I start? At the beginning, I suppose. My name is Gracie, I'm 20, and just like any other ordinary adolescent girl.

Except that I'm not.

Yes, I'm mad about music, a fashion fan, and I love bingeing a boxset, or five. It's just that the bingeing is repetitive, I typically play the same selection of songs on a loop and my clothes have to **feel** good as well as look good.

That's because I'm autistic.

It's taken me eons to commit to that statement and, if I'm honest, it's still scary saying it out loud.

When I first started writing the book you're now holding, I was planning on using an alias. Even though I was diagnosed autistic at 15 years old, it's not something I've freely shared. Embarrassed as I am to admit, I've dreaded what people will think of me.

While I might feel special and unique, in a mostly good way, I've found not everyone is open-minded or accepting around difference. In my experience, autism can be used as a bit of an insult, especially at school and among peers.

Act a bit wooden? You're autistic. Struggle socially? Autistic. Show an unusually keen interest in something? (Yes, you, Harry Potter!) Definitely on the spectrum.

As I can't recall hearing 'autistic' used positively in a sentence around the school corridors, I wasn't keen to draw negative attention towards myself by owning up to this book — not after years of masking, pretending to be 'normal' to fit in, avoiding the bullies and people-pleasing.

But over the last few months, things have changed. I'm at university. I've finally found friends who like me for who I am. Yes, my parents are frequent visitors, but I have actually left home, and I'm mostly fending for myself – things I never thought I would be capable of.

With a little time and space, I've mustered up the courage to not only process but also share what it was like to be an autistic girl in a secondary school setting. Succinctly? Traumatic! To the point, that some of us may never be able to cope with standard educational systems (more later). And that's okay.

Navigating the minefield that is social interactions, sensory overload and staying engaged in class means school can seriously suck, particularly when your brain is wired differently. But learning, however you choose to do it, is a vital factor in our young lives.

As autistic females we need and deserve to be educated, to learn and grow academically, socially and emotionally, gaining the skills to function and live autonomously and successfully. That should **never** be too much to ask.

That's why, for me, this is more than a book. It's a tool, for all you autistic adolescent girls in secondary schools who feel you've not been heard, whether you tend to go unnoticed, or get plenty of attention in negative ways.

I truly hope that you see yourselves in the scenarios I describe, and share this book with those who want and need to understand what it's like to be autistic, whether that's your family, friends or staff at your school.

Honestly, you are **not** alone. You **are** amazing. May the following pages help you to see, hear and feel that.

A QUICK NOTE ON TERMINOLOGY

You might have noticed I'm using the words 'autism' and 'autistic'. You've probably heard loads of terms such as 'autism spectrum condition' (ASC), 'high-functioning autism' and 'Asperger Syndrome'.

Since 2013, the medical diagnosis manual (the *Diagnostic and Statistical Manual of Mental*

Disorders, Fifth Edition, or DSM-5) has placed all these sub-categories under the umbrella term 'autism spectrum disorder' (ASD). However, I'm siding with autism expert Dr Luke Beardon and steering well clear of what I see as damaging labels. 'Disorders' and 'conditions' are reductive terms, branding us in a negative way.

Like Luke, I'm using PNT (predominant neurotype) to refer to the non-autistic population, rather than the more commonly adopted 'neurotypical'. To me, 'typical' carries connotations of 'the norm'. Autistic people are not abnormal but, as Luke wisely states, 'delightfully "autistically normal"'.

I have also chosen to use identify-first language, referring to myself and others as autistic, rather than individuals with autism. Autism isn't a shameful add-on, but a power that I have chosen to embrace. Of course, I respect people's rights to self-identify, and encourage checking out what linguistic forms individuals are happiest with.

CHAPTER 1

Understanding autism

Since my diagnosis, it's fair to say that I've developed a special interest in the subject – it's an autism thing! I've read countless books, scoured social media for blogs and vlogs, and even plucked up the courage to speak to (okay, email!) experts to understand what's going on with my autistic brain.

Because it's all about the brain, how our grey matter processes stuff.

This includes the way we communicate and relate to others – I can find socializing and interaction toe-curlingly challenging – and how we experience the world around us, particularly in sensory ways.

Like many autistic people, my behaviour can be rigid

and repetitive – say, stimming to soothe my anxiety (more of this later) or obsessively shopping on a theme. I'm currently investing heavily in Sylvanian Families (don't judge me), but I've also dropped huge funds on rings, sunglasses, bucket hats...you get the picture.

Next, just to dispel any myths, autism isn't 'catching' (I have actually been asked this question!). It's present from birth and with us for life. This doesn't mean it has to feel like a life sentence, though. My aim is for you to believe this by the time you finish reading this book.

Basically, while all autistic people share similar traits, we're all unique and will be affected in different ways. So, I'd 'kindly' ask the PNTs out there who label us as high- or low-functioning to stop. It minimizes our abilities and difficulties, and is just bloody rude.

Autism isn't static. How we feel fluctuates, usually depending on our environment. Top advice at my diagnosis included: see autism like a hi-fi system (or smart speaker). They all have similar settings, like volume control and choice of tone, but different ones are cranked up at different times in reaction to our surroundings.

Something else I've discovered is that it's three times more common for boys than girls to be diagnosed autistic. So much for equality! There are various explanations for this, such as the difference in our autistic traits. Boys may explode with frustration and anger while we might be more able to talk about difficult emotions (I said 'might').

Those special interests I've mentioned are more stereotypically autistic in boys – think planes, trains and computing – while ours fall into the more typical teen categories such as music, boxsets and fashion. It's not our passions that are unusual, just the amount of time we spend on them.

Additionally, the way autism is assessed has traditionally been based on male traits, meaning misdiagnosis or underdiagnosis for girls. It can be missed or eclipsed by other conditions, with doctors often seeing clumsiness (dyspraxia), poor attention (attention deficit hyperactivity disorder, ADHD) and mental health issues such as anorexia and self-harm rather than the autism underneath. As I know, this has seriously bad consequences.

Before I was finally identified as autistic, I experienced years of delays, clocking up a catalogue of diagnoses and a drawer full of medication for anxiety, clinical depression and post-traumatic stress disorder (PTSD). My autism remained missed and dismissed, including by one 'professional' who repeatedly insisted 'It's her nerves!' Now I'm no psychiatrist, but they definitely had issues.

Because of this, I felt like I was going mad. Dodgy diagnoses meant I was continually misunderstood and misinterpreted by my peers, my teachers, and even myself. The lack of support and compassion was distressing, leaving me feeling even more that I didn't fit in, despite trying so hard to do so.

Talking of which...

CHAPTER 2

Pretending to fit in

Ironically, the considerable effort we put into 'fitting in' by **masking** our autistic traits can lead to a later diagnosis for females. Before I define masking, I must clarify that I'm not an academic expert in the field. That said, I'm definitely a 'lived experience' expert on masking, seeing as I use it.

A lot.

The relief I felt when I heard the term and understood my everyday actions better was a proper eureka moment. Receiving a recent ADHD diagnosis (it's not uncommon for us to be multiply neurodivergent!) has helped me realize even more how I incessantly, and exhaustingly, modify my behaviours.

Masking, or camouflaging, is where we try to hide our

inherent autistic responses to social difficulties and sensory overload in an attempt to be accepted.

Methods include mimicking or copying the persona, mannerisms, interests and even speech patterns of others while editing out our autistic behaviours to seem 'normal'. The amount of jokes I've joined in the laughter for, even (often!) when I've failed to see the funny side, totally makes me cringe.

For me, masking is something I do consciously and subconsciously. I'm a bit like a behavioural detective, examining what others are doing and duplicating it to fit in socially. I call myself a chameleon, constantly changing, except it's not colours but my personality that I'm shifting to suit whatever situation I'm in.

Things I have done to mask, and that you might recognize in your own behaviours, include:

★ Holding eye contact and changing up facial expressions when I'm talking to someone. I usually have an internal ramble going on: 'Have I kept eye contact for long enough?' 'Do I need to smile or frown?' It's mentally challenging, rather like trying to balance a chemistry equation in your head, just harder.

★ Mirroring the body language of the person I'm talking to or borrowing the identity of someone I know PNTs admire, whether it's the popular kids around me or the latest Netflix sensation. (I often adopted an American accent in my primary years, having watched too many Disney channels.)

★ Scripting interactions. I've plotted out the many ways a conversation can go so I'm prepared for almost every eventuality. Memorizing friends' interests to slip into conversations (who doesn't like talking about themselves?) while limiting talking about my own (did I mention they can be intense?) seems to help the chat flow.

★ Stifling my sensory sensitivities to light, smell, touch and tastes, or avoiding stimming for fear of being labelled 'weird'.

These are just the tip of my autistic iceberg, strategies for sliding into the social norms, even though the rules make no sense. It can be torture. Like pretending you like something, even when you don't, that is, lying, something my parents told me not to engage in!

Birthdays were a nightmare when I was younger. Invariably I'd upset at least one friend or family member with my face, and sometimes words, showing the genuine disappointment I felt at the presents I'd been given.

The time my uncle gifted me a Hello Kitty alarm clock for my 13th birthday was a particular low. He thought it might help my chaotic brain 'master timekeeping'. I reminded him that I had a phone (and mum) for such matters, and that I didn't like pink. Or clocks. Or cats.

Mortified, my parents had to (re)educate me that in such situations we need to follow the social rules, which means sometimes 'fibbing' to save others' feelings. I had to educate them to strictly buy from my birthday list and show me my gifts before wrapping them. Like a lot of autistic people, I hate surprises. I'm much calmer if I know what to expect.

At primary school I was regularly called 'weird'. And 'different'. And 'difficult'. Not just by pupils, but parents, too. As quirky wasn't aspirational, I was bullied. Determined for things to be different at secondary school, I committed to masking.

I remember going proper TOWIE with my Essex accent around certain peer groups, just to appear cool, dropping my 't's and driving my mum mad in the process. I changed my sense of style, swapping my beloved baggy jeans for tight, branded leggings, which looked disgusting and gave me sensory overload.

I listened to music I hated just to fit in with my friends' choices. I'm sure he's a lovely guy, but even hearing Shawn Mendes' 'Stitches' now triggers a trauma response. I was desperate to belong, to never feel like an outcast again.

For a short while, it worked. I transformed myself into this popular individual with a 'great' group of mates. And then it bombed. Pretending to be someone I wasn't and not letting them get to know the real me seriously unsettled both camps. They accused me of being fake (fair point!), and I was burnt out from copying.

Burnout is a huge issue for us autistic girls trying to

navigate the social and sensory demands of school. When it hits, we're left physically and mentally exhausted. We're less able to manage life skills and even less tolerant of sensory stimulus.

Honestly, constantly muting our instinctive reactions is gruelling. Second-guessing responses while feeling terrified of getting 'found out' can make us seriously unhappy. We're internally battling against who we want and need to be. As I lost any sense of 'me', my self-esteem plummeted, increasing my anxiety, depression and meltdowns.

That's because masking doesn't drive out the underlying anxiety we feel at school. What's more, keeping it together all day in class means it's likely to leak out (**explode**) at home. I've smashed up my bedroom on more occasions than I'd like to remember, releasing the high levels of stress that I've worked so hard to hide during the school day.

This is why it's vital for anyone reading this who works in a school to (please!) believe families and parents sharing the chaos they're experiencing at home, even if it majorly contrasts with how calm autistic children, especially girls, can seem to be in the classroom. Not listening to parents and us feels harsh when you realize the impact masking has.

Of course, not everyone's tuned in to the female presentation of autism, so an awareness of typical autistic female traits (though everyone is different) is vital in supporting families, us and also school staff with identification (share this list with your teacher!!).

Common female autistic traits include:

★ Seeming shy, immature and out of touch with trends or social norms.

★ Being perceived as 'odd', leading to isolation or poor treatment by peers.

★ Staying on the edge of friendship groups, moving between them without joining in, or having one close friend you don't want to share.

★ Having intense interests and repetitive behaviours.

★ Sensory sensitivities, say, to light, sounds, smells, tastes and textures – comfy clothing might be your go-to.

★ Poor fine motor skills (the coordination of small muscle groups, like those in your hands and fingers) and gross motor skills (large muscle movements, like walking).

★ Stilted or unnatural speech.

★ Delays in responding when spoken to directly, because you need time to process language or to come up with a 'correct' response.

★ Getting anxious when asked to perform in social situations and avoiding answering questions because you're scared of getting things wrong.

★ Falling grades, or, perhaps, consistent A* grades – the pursuit for perfectionism, driven by a rigid need for control, plus the fear of not meeting impossible standards and garnering disapproval, can lead to burnout.

★ Different personas in different settings – perhaps you're quiet and withdrawn in class but have major meltdowns when you stop masking and release those bottled-up emotions at home.

★ Exhaustion from trying to decipher social rules and masking to hide your differences.

If you recognize yourself in this list and are desperate for others to begin the process of understanding you, shove it under their noses. Then do your best to be yourself. Yes, you'll still use masking, particularly when you're anxious, but it's okay to show, and embrace, the true you, too. Love your uniqueness – and lean into it.

CHAPTER 3

Managing sensory sensitivities and the risk of overload

Like many autistic girls, I can majorly struggle processing everyday sensory information, say, different noises, smells, light, touch or tastes. Sensory stuff that's hardly noticeable for PNTs can be **unbearable** for us.

Any of our senses can be over- (hyper-) or under- (hypo-) sensitive, depending on the moment. If you're hypersensitive to temperature, you might radically react to heat, stripping off layers at the first beam of sun, or fashion your duvet into an overcoat as the frost hits. The temperature hyposensitive among us can be seen modelling shorts and tees in arctic conditions ('No, for the gazillionth time, I do not feel cold').

For me, certain taste and texture challenges have designated my diet bland, beige and repetitive. Shout out to my Irish roots for the humble potato. In school, bright strip lighting hurt my eyes, mustering migraines, the bell rattled my brain, and strong canteen smells set off my gag reflex.

Touch can either soothe or **really** irritate me. I love having my hair brushed and my head and neck firmly massaged. Hugs, **if** I allow them, must be strong, and I like my baths flesh-meltingly hot. But certain tickly sensations aggravate me. Wispy strands of hair on my face or a soft touch on my arm feel like they're bruising my skin and certain fabrics – well, clothes – have always been a nightmare.

I refused to wear tights (the clue's in the word) until secondary school, and only then did so because the discomfort of not fitting in was worse than the excruciating cling of 60 denier. I cut out all labels from my shirts, skirt and blazer (so scratchy!), which was better for my skin, but not my parents' bank balance.

My ADHD means I'm prone to 'misplacing' things, so locating my kit in the school lost property mountain was virtually impossible. I tried once. The whiff of 'lost' trainers was overpowered by the smell of sick. The sick was mine. As I'm emetophobic (throwing up = panic attack), I became hysterical. I was sent home (yay!).

I also suffered daily breakdowns over my school tie, which was both restrictive and a nightmare to tie when your fine motor skills resemble those of a toddler. Basically, school is a brutal environment for us autistic kids. It's so full of noise. People. Sudden changes.

From the moment we enter the gates we're surrounded by chaos, be it navigating our way across packed playgrounds, pushing through crammed corridors, or attending crowded assemblies. Factor in crushing canteen queues with vile smells, splitting sounds and blinding lights, and you have the type of sensory saturation that triggers meltdowns and shutdowns (more later), particularly when combined with processing problems.

Fellow autistic author Siena Castellon also highlights

the mental overwhelm we experience. There are endless unwritten social rules that govern lunchtime interactions – where you sit...who to talk to...when to talk...what about... (Aggghhh!)

So, how to manage it? Well, we can't change our brains. It's therefore vital for schools to switch up the environment, to make it a less harsh and exhausting place for us.

Need some suggestions to wave at senior leaders? Here you go...

★ Change should start in classrooms. Are the walls cluttered with displays? Is the temperature tropical or arctic? Is it noisy or overcrowded? I get that you're trying to cater for 'everyone' but they're not meeting neurodiverse needs. And that's not inclusive.

Challenging conditions land us in a sensory spin. This makes learning almost impossible. Dr Luke Beardon recommends completing a sensory profile for every autistic student and tweaking the environment.

★ Offer respite. Giving us 'time out' cards means

we can leave class to decompress when we're overstimulated.

★ Let us leave lessons five minutes early. It helps us avoid the end of lesson crush and benefit from empty, calm corridors on the way to our next class.

★ Silence the school bell. The sudden shrieking is majorly distressing.

★ Get creative, providing quiet spaces for when we need time alone. Professor Francesca Happé suggests letting us sort books in the library or allowing us to wear earplugs or headphones if noise is too much. A sensory room with soft lights, chilled sounds and regulating textures can soothe the senses.

★ Stagger canteen sittings. This limits our exposure to noise and crowds. Or encourage autistic students to bring a packed lunch to eat in a quiet space.

★ Bend the rules on uniform. Letting us undo a top button or loosen (or take off!) our ties won't leave us disregarding behaviour policies and running feral in the corridors.

As well as needing environmental tweaks, I carry a self-soothing kit for when my senses are assaulted. Using a cosmetic bag is subtle enough not to draw unwanted attention. Mine is filled with things to calm me down, including:

★ Essential oils. I'm a fan of lavender's soothing properties, plus the pleasing smell helps drown out the less pleasant ones around school.

★ Fiddle toys. These help me regulate when I'm overloaded. There are some great spiky acupressure rings online, which are ideal for twiddling and again, are understated enough to go unnoticed in class.

★ Earbuds. Ideal for dampening down or blocking out noise and playing tunes to calm me down.

★ Bach Rescue Remedy® spray or pastels. Just the action of spritzing my tongue or popping a pastel in my mouth helps me feel I'm doing something proactive to ease my anxiety.

★ Chewing gum. The repetitive motion of chewing helps with sensory integration and makes me feel relaxed, but focused.

★ Snack bar. We can struggle processing feelings of hunger or thirst. I often forget or leave it too late to eat. Carrying a snack reduces my 'hangry' outbursts.

CHAPTER 4

Clear communication and making friends

Having continued difficulties with interacting and communicating socially is a biggie for us autistic girls. We can struggle making sense of both speech and body language, using or interpreting facial expressions, tuning into tone of voice, as well as jokes and sarcasm. I mostly think people mean exactly what they say, making me embarrassingly gullible, and an excellent target for wind-ups.

I aced the 'taking things literally' component of my diagnosis when the lovely lady assessing me explained how tricky it is for us to 'read people'. I frankly informed her that with no pages, it wasn't just tricky, but 'impossible'. What she meant was, it's hard for us to pick up on others' emotions or intentions.

It's also a minefield expressing our own. Like me, perhaps you've been labelled 'blunt', 'weird', 'socially inept' or just 'bloody rude', particularly if you're banging on about your latest intense interests. A lag in processing skills also means we can look bored or like we're not listening during conversations.

I've been told that I have a 'resting bitch face'. It's not something I've worked hard to perfect. I'm just taking a bit of extra time to decipher what it is that someone is actually saying.

Again, these challenges are a total nightmare, slowing or blocking our progress academically and socially. While there's no magic bullet, there are ways staff can (**should**) go about supporting us, both in and out of class. This list is for your teachers!

★ Get our attention. Use our names at the start of sentences so we know you're addressing us.

★ Use a filter. Too much information causes overload. Sift out less important stuff, and stress or repeat the key facts.

★ Go slow. Pause between phrases. This gives us time to digest what you've said and come back with a decent answer.

★ Ask the **right** questions. With so many possible answers, open-ended questions fry our brains. Keep queries short and specific.

★ Err on the literal side. You do you with sarcasm, exaggeration and weird figures of speech and expect us to do us. We will take you at your word (yes, I have physically pulled my socks up!) unless you tell otherwise.

★ Show and tell. Visual aids such as timetables, mind maps and flow charts are great for breaking down what you want us to know.

★ Get to know us. Headteacher of Limpsfield Grange School, Sarah Wild, says that a daily check-in at the start of school with a chosen adult is time really well spent. It helps us manage our anxieties about the day. Asking what does and doesn't work for us can help you understand why we act in certain ways.

Examples include:

★ I look away when you are talking to me so I can properly concentrate on what you're saying.

★ I hate raised voices and shouting. It makes me think I'm in trouble, and I can't focus on what's being said.

★ Processing stuff takes time. I'm not being rude or lazy when I don't instantly answer.

★ Small talk isn't my strong point, but I'm still (mostly!) interested in what you're saying.

★ I often say what I think without editing first. Sorry!

FRIENDSHIPS

It won't land as a shock when I say making and keeping friends is flipping tough for autistic females. Granted, we're typically more sociable than autistic males, but boy do we struggle in the PNT 'relational' world.

I have had **so** many 'friendships'. The majority have been disastrous, causing untold agony to myself and my family who have relentlessly soothed me through the battlefield of peer relations. I've made some really poor choices. Desperate to 'fit in', I've entered social situations, checked out the top dogs and queen bees, and copied their behaviours, good or bad.

I still can't block out the memory of 13-year-old me, dancing in my front garden, in a bikini, in December, because my 'friend' said it would be 'a laugh'. The neighbours heard the ear-splitting music long before they noticed my unseasonal attire. The shame was worth no level of 'belonging'.

Thankfully, ageing has helped me to (mostly) realize what's good for me, what to avoid, and who to gravitate towards. Personally, I cope well in male company. Sure, boys can be total tools, but I find them less complex than a lot of females. Disputes pass quickly and cleanly, while the psychological warfare accompanying female conflict feels relentless.

Having said that, I have a few amazing girlfriends now. Interestingly, we've all been on the nasty end of mean-girl behaviours. We therefore 'get' and support each other.

Branching outside my immediate peer group has been

beneficial, especially mixing with older students who seem more mature. It's worth targeting those with shared interests, too. In my experience, if you want to find someone who matches or out-quirks you, the drama department is a good place to start.

Having friendships out of school has also been a lifesaver, providing a breath of fresh air away from an intense setting with multiple agendas. I'm appreciated for being me. And that feels good.

Still, school's the place we spend the most time. Here, friendships can be distressing and tiring when you **do** understand the social rules. For the neurodiverse, they're quadruply agonizing and exhausting. We therefore need to educate the educators on better supporting our bonding abilities.

Here goes:

★ Recognize autistic patterns in friendships. We can be fixated on one person or on a couple of close friends. This feels intense for all concerned. It can create conflict, something we're rubbish at managing.

Headteacher Sarah Wild recommends unpicking social interactions in real time, to help us grasp what's going on. A running commentary helps; for example, 'This is why this person did this and reacted like that', supports our understanding and limits blow-ups.

★ Create a safe space. While encouraging a wide circle of friends can help reduce the intensity felt with just a few, time alone is vital. Socializing drains our emotional and intellectual batteries, triggering what Dr Luke Beardon, I think, very aptly calls 'social hangovers'. We then become burnt out, additionally triggered by sensory stuff and less able to function.

That's why school staff need to make it okay and normal for us to retreat when we're physically and mentally exhausted, providing quiet spaces for alone time. For me this was the inclusion unit. As soon as Ms G & B saw me enter, the kettle went on so I could simultaneously gulp down hot chocolate and biscuits while dropping the F-bomb.

★ Provide structure. 'Loose' times like lunchtime or breaktime are danger zones. Crowded canteens, playground pandemonium, plus the unpredictability of other people's behaviours are major anxiety triggers. Ways of bringing structure to the unstructured include:

- Lunchtime clubs. Author of *Educating and Supporting Autistic Girls* Victoria Honeybourne recommends establishing distinct guidelines for group work, allocating specific roles so that everyone is clear about expectations from the get-go. Throwing myself into Drama Club helped give my day structure. Sharing interests was a great foundation for friendships, too.

- Breaktime supervision. Staff can help us express our feelings if we're struggling, plus it limits the bullying that can occur when things aren't monitored.

BULLYING

As I type 'bullying', all sorts of emotions bubble up for me. First, shame. What if those who've bullied me, or the adults I asked for help, read this and insist I'm 'over-reacting', 'too sensitive' and 'making it up' –

just like they did at the time? That feels doubly invalidating.

I don't want to be overdramatic (another label!), but bullying is painful and traumatizing. At primary school, my table 'mates' announced that they were going to play a game where 'We don't talk to Gracie for an hour'. As I expectantly enquired whether the hour was up, I was told, 'Oh, it's a day now.' The next day, 24 hours had been extended to a week.

Secondary school was worse. Two individuals conducted a 'fun' survey asking: 'Who hates Gracie?' They kept a growing tally on their clipboard. When the teacher challenged them, they innocently responded that they were only joking! Hilarious.

I couldn't even escape it once home. Thanks to modern tech, fake Instagram accounts were set up in my name, like the one with pictures of me captioned 'more despised than Hitler'.

Of course, tech isn't all bad. Co-editor of *Girls and Autism* Jo Egerton suggests joining an online autism community when you feel alone (try X's #actuallyautistic), or bonding with others who experience the world in a similar way. However, ultimately, bullying sucks.

If your teachers say, 'It doesn't happen here', don't believe them. Bullying happens at all schools. It's cruel and unacceptable, and you are not to blame.

Knowing the facts might help you and your family to challenge the deniers.

BULLYING: THE FACTS

There's no legal definition of bullying, but the Anti-Bullying Alliance describe it as: 'The repetitive, intentional hurting of one person or group by another person or group, where the relationship involves an imbalance of power.'

Bullying can be physical, verbal or psychological, and it can happen in person or online.

Examples of bullying I've experienced include:

- Being called names, insulted, threatened or humiliated.

- Others making stuff up to get me into trouble.

- Having false rumours spread about me in person and online.

- Receiving silent phone calls and getting abusive texts.

- Getting my belongings trashed.

- Being persistently excluded from social groups or ignored.

Anti-Bullying Alliance, https://anti-bullyingalliance. org.uk/tools-information/all-about-bullying/ understanding-bullying/definition

The impact of bullying is not pretty. I've experienced anxiety and depression and refused to go to school. My peers brushed off my two weeks' absence, rumouring that I was 'in a mental institution'. I wasn't. I was lying in my dark bedroom, too scared to get up and too sad to engage with anyone apart from my trusty golden retriever, who loved me unconditionally.

Burnt out, it wasn't that I wouldn't go to school. I couldn't. Author Eliza Fricker writes about this brilliantly in her book, *Can't Not Won't*. She details her daughter's daily tears and traumatic reactions to attending mainstream school, as well as her heavy parental guilt.

Reading it, my mum and I remembered the time she faked having my headmaster on the phone. She said he was getting in his car...to take me to school...in my pyjamas. I chose the less humiliating option of letting my mum wrestle me into my uniform, spending the rest of the day, near-catatonic in class, willing the final bell to ring.

My mum feels truly awful about this. She describes having 'run out of ideas', not knowing what to do for the best. Desperate, we even tried another secondary school. While I was told they understood and could support my needs, my first day resulted in what I felt to be a painful public humiliation.

I was reprimanded for rolling my skirt up. I wasn't rebelling or breaking the rules on purpose. It was the last one in the shop and it was too big for me, so I was trying to stop it falling down. I was too overwhelmed to explain this at the time, and I am not sure it mattered because I was breaking the school 'rules'. Anyway, I refused to attend the detention. Or the school again.

Sadly, as a lot of autistic girls find with mainstream schools, it failed to meet my needs.

It wasn't until I was paired with a magnificent member of staff who fully believed me, fighting my corner and giving me a voice, that I got back to my old school. I'd therefore urge you to seek out a truly trusted person, someone from your family, a teacher, or a friend to confide in and provide support.

When it comes to combating bullying, I've been given umpteen strategies over the years. Some are more effective than others...

★ Seek out a safe space and swerve what Siena Castellon calls 'bullying hotspots'. So much bullying happens at breaktimes. You're an easy target when there's less staff around to monitor things. Position yourself near the adults on duty and avoid unsupervised spaces, such as stairwells and toilets. Joining a club can help those in charge keep an eye on you.

★ Just ignore them. Yes, I know, easier said than done! But giving bullies a reaction is as dangerous as throwing petrol on a fire. Be assertive, tell them to stop, but, for your own safety, don't fight back.

★ Please remember, this is **not** your fault. Repetitive attacks can really make you believe you deserve it, but, as Siena says, no one should be bullied, whoever they are, no matter how they look, or what their race, sexuality or culture is.

★ Know your rights. All schools have an anti-bullying policy. Reading up on those, as well as some online resources, will help you feel more empowered (go to the FYI section at the end of the book).

STAYING SAFE

Okay, so I wasn't sure where to put this in the book. Or whether to mention it at all, especially with the thought of my teachers reading this. However, it's a hot topic of conversation, featuring pretty heavily at school.

I'm talking about **sex.**

There, I've said it. I'm not going to go into the ins and outs (lol) of it, but I won't pretend it doesn't happen either.

When I write 'staying safe', I'm not just thinking about contraception, although condoms are vital if you want to avoid both unwanted pregnancy and sexually transmitted infections (STIs). I'm thinking about physical and emotional safety, too.

Remember what I said about being gullible? Well, autistic girls can be naive and easily deceived. We're at risk of abuse, feeling peer pressured into unsafe behaviours, just to fit in and be liked. I know this to my cost.

Full disclosure feels, well, too exposing here. Let's just say, I've rushed things on the intimacy front, racing through milestones while not having the emotional maturity to back it up. As the saying goes, 'we live and learn'. I guess I'm feeling a bit protective over you all and encouraging you not to hit boiling point on the regret-ometre.

All schools have a duty of care in providing sex education, but some extra knowledge might help you to properly decide whether you're ready or not:

★ Know the law. The age of consent for any sexual activity is 16. The law isn't there to persecute under-16s engaged in mutually consenting, non-abusive, sexual activity. It's there to protect children from abuse, stating that any 12-years-old or younger are unable to legally consent to any sexual activity (Sexual Offences Act 2003).

★ Take other people's stories with a bucket of salt. Just because everyone says they're doing 'it' doesn't mean they are – or that you have to.

★ Follow what, and who, feels right for you. Being pressured, worried that you'll be dumped if you don't, or scared of hurting someone's feelings are not the right reasons to have sex.

★ Having sex doesn't mean you're going to live 'happily ever after' with a significant other. You're at school. You won't be with this person for the rest of your life. Sex won't make them fall in love with you, or you with them for that matter (I told you I could be blunt!).

CHAPTER 5

Learning hurdles and how to jump them

At the start of this book, I mentioned 'learning' as one of the key reasons we go to school. Studying different subjects is supposed to give us the knowledge and skills we need to independently progress in life. Throwing in the hormonal minefield and boundary-pushing behaviours of adolescence complicates this.

Add in autism, and you've got a total car crash.

Sensory overload, issues with processing information and typically spikey profiles, which means we may excel in some subjects but bomb others (third time lucky for my maths GCSE, thank you!) means getting an education is exhausting. Science nerds have 'catchily' identified our challenges as being with 'executive functioning'.

EXECUTIVE FUNCTIONING

I promise to go slow here...

> Autism effects the frontal lobes
> (zones!) of our brains.

> These areas are responsible for
> executive functioning.

> Executive functioning (EF) is the group
> of abilities that help us handle our
> thoughts, emotions and actions.

> This is so we get things done.

These 'things' include organizing,
planning and managing tasks.

Our skills plummet offline when
we're tired, ill, stressed or overloaded
by social and sensory stuff.

As PNTs don't always understand what's going on,
they might judge us lazy, defeatist, belligerent or just
plain stupid — why could we do something yesterday,
but not today? Because of EF! (and the environment).
We're not making excuses, just struggling to get
tasks on track.

The infuriating challenges we face are:

★ Organizing our thoughts.

★ Poor concentration and staying focused, except
when we're really into something.

★ Planning and prioritizing.

★ Independently getting started on stuff and then managing to finish it.

★ Following instructions, particularly if there are too many steps.

★ Picking out important points from less relevant information.

★ Moving from one piece of work to another.

★ Poor short-term memory – that's stuff that happened in the last seven seconds!

★ Poor working memory – that's being able to keep information in mind while we're working on it.

★ Impulsivity.

★ Self-reflection – we struggle recognizing our strengths and weaknesses and how to make improvements next time.

So what can schools, and we ourselves, do to help?

THINGS SCHOOLS CAN DO

★ Make learning 'concrete'. Show us **how** to do something rather than bombarding us with abstract ideas.

★ Be visual. Visual timetables help us see what's coming, providing routine and predictability for the day. Mind maps and flow charts help us organize information, and highlight important stuff, like instructions for a test.

★ Limit overwhelm by breaking tasks down into smaller chunks. We're more likely to follow and finish instructions if there are fewer per page.

★ Provide pre-learning. We're better able to contribute in class if you tell us what's coming up.

★ Remember our special interests! You'll hold our focus if we're fascinated by something.

★ Update us on changes. Consistency and routine help us feel safe and ready to learn. Last-minute timetable changes are terrifying. If you can't give us warning, at least check that we're okay.

THINGS WE CAN DO

★ Siena Castellon recommends colour coding textbooks and files to correspond with a colour-coded timetable – say, purple for maths and red for English – which worked well for me. It helps you keep track of what you need for each lesson.

★ Make lists. They help with prioritizing and reminders, and it's a buzz ticking stuff off. A notebook is fine, although I jot things on my phone, as I'm less likely to lose it.

★ Double up. If I'm not losing stuff, I'm forgetting it. Having duplicates, like a compass set, at home and school, has saved me racking up negative points from narky teachers.

★ Set alarms and alerts. They're great as reminders and help with planning how much time to spend on a task.

★ Create a stress-free study space. If you can't limit noise, use earbuds. A clear desk and phone-free zone boosts concentration.

MOTOR SKILLS

This isn't about knowing your way around a car engine or pulling a handbrake turn. Rather, motor skills are when we move specific muscles to perform everyday tasks. And guess what? The autistic brain can be compromised here.

Fine motor skills help us make precise movements with our fingers and hands – so, writing, adjusting a microscope or using a compass in maths. Personally, I have a nightmare with buttons, zips, tying my shoelaces and navigating cutlery, etc. I still can't unsee my classmates' horrified reactions to me slicing veg with a bread knife in food tech.

PE has always been challenging. In spite of always pre-lacing my trainers to reduce getting-dressed time, it never made up for my poor gross motor skills. These govern our larger muscles in the arms, legs and torso, and relate to body awareness, speed, balance and strength.

Tragically, I can fall over a flat pavement and a ball never goes in the direction I think I'm throwing it (I was often 'ill' on sports day). As I've no ambition to represent my country at the Olympics, I can live with this. But getting my education is non-negotiable.

The best adaptation for me has been using a laptop. At school, I sat with an educational psychologist, writing out paragraphs – not for punishment, but to gauge my speed. It was that of a 10-year-old. I can't do joined-up (cursive) writing, and what I do write is illegible.

Typing has been a lifesaver. I agree with Dr Luke Beardon that there's no point getting us to spend relentless hours developing a skill like handwriting if we're not going to use it in the long run. Just let us use laptops!

RELATIONSHIP BUILDING

Along with the practical stuff that aids learning, building a supportive relationship with a staff member who can fight your corner is essential. Headteacher Sarah Wild, first urges schools to ask **us** who we want to work with. If the wrong person is offering the support, the support won't work!

Next, provide a safe space and time for teachers to really get to know us. Find out what we're into, and accept and celebrate us for who we are.

Check in frequently, too. Ask if we understand what's being taught, and whether we're struggling behind the scenes. This is because we're people-pleasers.

We hate inconveniencing anyone, and the thought of upsetting or riling our teachers with 'rubbish' work feels excruciating. This means we often go above and beyond what's expected, exhausting ourselves, triggering burnout.

I spent four days, and a lot of tears, writing a media essay that should have taken a few hours. The resources might as well have been written in Japanese (I'm not fluent). While my mum told me to 'just leave it', I became upset and furious shouting, 'I have to get an A*'.

My teacher was delighted with the result, but had no idea what I'd been through. Until my mum told her. That's the thing. Teachers aren't mind readers.

We, or our advocates, need to tell teachers what's

going on, otherwise they reach their own conclusions, some of which aren't helpful, or kind. I've known teachers to be properly blinkered as our actions don't match their expectations of what autism is. We often act like model students, so we can be overlooked or pressured to 'fit in'.

I had one teacher rejecting my diagnosis, suggesting, I was 'making it up'. I was clearly using it as an 'excuse' for being stroppy (meltdowns!) and rude (shutdowns!) because a lot of the time I appeared 'perfectly normal' (masking!). These sort of ignorant assumptions have led to PNT expectations being loaded on me.

Teachers can pressure us to 'fit in' and be more like the other kids. They expect us to get on with things, even when we're totally overwhelmed by overstimulating environments. Again, this is why that one understanding, compassionate and accepting relationship is crucial.

For me, my key worker was a blessing. She took time to learn what I could and couldn't cope with. She then told all my subject teachers, so they knew too. Thank you, Mel G.

HOMEWORK

Ah, homework. The trigger for tears, explosions and shutdowns. After a long school day spending all our energy learning, masking and filtering out sensory irritants, it's no surprise we've nothing left to give.

Homework can rule and ruin family life. Not only are we knackered, but issues with processing instructions, gauging how long to spend on tasks (remember EF?!) and often a need to be perfect sparks major anxiety before we've even put pen to paper (or fingers to keyboard).

I can't promise to take this all away, and truthfully, there are times when homework should seriously be suspended for the sake of us managing the rest of the school day.

If you can face it, the following **might** soothe study time:

Teachers

★ Give precise instructions of what needs to be

done, and by when. Providing a checklist of materials needed helps.

★ Bullet points help break down information, while flow charts give a visual map for navigating tasks.

★ Use multiple choice questions to test knowledge rather than setting long, overwhelming assignments.

Parents or carers

★ Discuss whether your daughter needs a break when she's home, or prefers to get things out of the way.

★ Stick to this predictable structure, and sort a space free from distractions, like TVs and phones.

★ Help! Author of *The Girl with the Curly Hair: Asperger's and Me*, Alis Rowe, says collaborating on planning and prioritizing before starting tasks reduces overwhelm.

★ Setting a timer is a great visual cue for how long your daughter needs to study.

You

★ Keep it at school. Ask teachers to study supervised, there, limiting stress at home.

★ Be creative. When my brain was mashed by 'studying', watching DVDs of plays set for English/Drama helped. YouTube videos are great for tutoring you through most subjects.

★ Good enough is good enough. Author of *From Hurt to Hope*, Mair Elliott, says, 'Perfection, or trying to achieve it, doesn't bring happiness... Your worth does not hinge on being perfect.'

EXAMS

I hate exams. So much. To the point that I could fill another book on just how much I loathe them.

I know I'm not alone in this and that you don't have to be autistic to detest tests and exams. The pressure to remember all you've learned over the last couple of years and then spew it out under timed conditions can trigger anyone's anxiety.

For me, my rigid need to be perfect paralysed me before I even started revising. Even now, I have this weird logic that if I don't do anything and fail, it's better than doing something and it not being good enough, and then proving I'm not perfect by failing.

EF issues meant I struggled with planning, prioritizing and working out what was important from reams of revision notes. By the time I reached the exam room my panic was stratospheric. Shaking, I pored over the paper, aware that my literal understanding of questions affected how I answered them.

Throw in sensory overload from the vast hall, strip lighting, sniffing, shuffling students and intimidating invigilators pacing between the desks, and I was reduced to a mad woman. A mad woman who was expected to produce work reflecting her true academic abilities and results that would enable her to move on to the next deserved step of her education and ultimately fulfil her potential as an independent working adult.

All I can say (politely) is, 'Not. Fair.' Still, while this ridiculous system of testing exists, it looks like we've got to work with it. Clearly, I don't have all the answers (although exams would certainly be easier if I did), but I tried to harness my hysteria in the following ways:

★ See the bigger picture. It's grating having to show what we know about stuff that we'll never use in the big wide world (yes, you, algebra!). Still, my teachers and parents helped me see learning as small steps towards my final destination.

If you want to go to uni, you have to get your A-Levels, which means having decent GCSEs to make sixth form, which means choosing strong options, etc., etc., etc. (On a lighter note, I picked a degree where assessments are based on course work, not exams. Clever, huh?!)

★ Rehearse. Exams put a rocket up our normal school routine. Getting teachers to talk and walk you through the logistics, when and where exams will take place, helps in managing expectations.

★ Practice makes...good enough. It helps knowing what to expect. Because we often take things literally and struggle with open-ended questions, working through past papers with teachers to understand the wording and what's being asked helps.

★ Work to your strengths. As my GCSEs got closer, I focused on my strongest subjects, those I wanted to study moving forward, easing off on the ones that weren't clicking (sorry, science teachers!). Speak to school about what you can manage, and sit the number of exams that feels right for you.

★ Prepare, to pass. Structure your studies with a timetable, prioritizing what to revise and when. Pencil in time for breaks, drinks, exercise, etc., to reduce stress, and stay positive.

Consider also:

When are you up – with the larks, or are you more nocturnal in your study style?

Where do you focus best – at home, school, the library, or a coffee shop?

Who would you benefit from – a study buddy? Or do you prefer to go solo?

What you need – revision guides, past papers, Post-it® notes, highlighter pens...

SPECIAL ARRANGEMENTS FOR EXAMS

Having a diagnosis means many of us are entitled to access arrangements for external exams. Schools can apply for these in advance. It usually involves being assessed by a specialist teacher or educational psychologist.

Benefits include:

★ Extra time. My focus isn't great. I struggle weighing up how much time to spend on questions. Before getting extra time, I never finished a paper and always felt like a failure. More minutes give space to process instructions and understand questions. You might also benefit from a prompter sitting with you, monitoring your progress and keeping you on track.

★ A separate room. Sensory issues abound in big exam halls. Smaller rooms where you can sit alone or with less students help reduce distractions.

★ A laptop. Remember those poor fine motor skills? Slow, illegible writing is not conducive to acing exams. Find out if you're entitled to a laptop or even a scribe to support you.

★ Supervised rest breaks. If you become increasingly overwhelmed or can't focus, the clock can be stopped for an agreed period of time, allowing you headspace out of the room.

CHAPTER 6

Autism and additional diagnoses

I don't want to appear greedy, but I'm not just autistic. I also have ADHD and dyspraxia, and I'm hypermobile. It's pretty common to have co-occurring conditions, so connections should be quickly considered to ensure we get the right support.

ADHD

While just over a decade ago ADHD and ASD were seen as being mutually exclusive, many specialists now believe having both conditions is common. It's even birthed its own label, AuDHD, with YouTuber Samantha Stein (@SamanthaSStein) highlighting its contradiction – the need for rigid routines combined with an inability to maintain structure!

I only received my ADHD diagnosis after a term at uni. When my mum let herself into my student flat, she thought I'd been burgled. It was a fair assumption. My room appeared ransacked – clothes, lecture notes and takeaway cartons covered the floor.

I was too anxious to go to the laundrette, couldn't organize my studies, missing multiple deadlines, and struggled breaking down recipes to cook from scratch. The emotional and practical scaffolding my family provided at home had gone.

My autism had taken centre stage at school, and because there's a crossover in traits, my ADHD was missed. Retrospectively, all the signs were there. You might recognize some:

- ★ Daydreaming in class and missing information.

- ★ Forgetful and always losing stuff.

- ★ Trouble paying and shifting attention from one task to another, following instructions and finishing work.

- ★ Totally disorganized (messy mind = messy school bag).

★ Poor time management and queen of procrastination.

★ Feeling restless, fidgeting or filling exercise books with doodles.

★ Excessive chat and cutting others off in conversation.

★ Very emotional and quick to cry.

★ Socially awkward and struggle forming friendships.

★ Poor self-care and haphazard hygiene habits.

★ Low self-esteem.

★ Underachievement.

Again, ADHD is a brain thing. Compared to PNTs we have lower levels of two neurotransmitters (dopamine and noradrenaline) that spark attention and help you feel rewarded. The results are a lack of focus and/or the pursuit of a buzz.

ADHD medication has upped my focus and reduced my impulsivity. I can now read a page once (okay, maybe twice) rather than 20 times to get the information.

Other strategies you could try to get through school include:

★ Chunking tasks into smaller parts. Writing a 1500-word essay or solving 30 maths equations in one sitting is overwhelming. Set smaller targets, like writing a paragraph or completing five questions. Then take a brain break.

★ Move. Poor concentration triggers fidgeting. Doodling can improve your focus, while brief breaks to stretch and walk around relieve restlessness.

★ Limit distractions. Ask to be seated away from the door and windows (too much to stare at!). Wearing earbuds can tune out noise, too.

★ Sleep well. Not in class (although I have been known to drop off), but at home. Racing thoughts, hyperactivity and nightmares mean sleep can be scant for us ADHDers, leaving us too knackered to learn the next day. Following the acronym **SCREEN** can help:

S = Screen. Limit screen time, turning off TVs/

games consoles/tablets/phones an hour before bed.

C = Caffeine. Cut out caffeinated drinks after lunchtime.

R = Routine. Establish an enjoyable bedtime routine, taking a relaxing warm bath or re-reading your favourite book.

E = Exercise. Have regular exercise three hours before bedtime. Expose yourself to morning daylight to reset your body clock.

E = Eat a healthy diet. Try to limit sugar and E numbers.

N = Say 'No' to smoking, alcohol and illegal drugs.

DYSPRAXIA

As mentioned, I can fall over a flat pavement. Poor pen grip means my writing is illegible, and I still eat with toddler cutlery in the privacy of my own home.

Thanks to dyspraxia (also known as developmental coordination disorder, or DCD) I've been labelled 'clumsy', 'awkward' and a 'danger to myself' (and others).

As dyspraxia disrupts the messages sent between the brain (!!) and body, it hampers fine and gross motor skills, and impacts our ability to plan and organize stuff, too. Poor spatial awareness means I'm frequently bumping into stuff and, although I miraculously passed my driving test, I still can't parallel park.

If you recognize the following, you may be dyspraxic:

★ Frequently collide with people and things.

★ Lose balance easily, and trip and fall a lot.

★ PE is your nemesis, especially activities that require good hand–eye coordination, like throwing and catching.

★ Difficulties following instructions and keeping up in class.

★ Poor pen or pencil grip and writing slowly and illegibly.

★ Struggle with handling equipment, like cutting with scissors or using a locker key.

Small adaptations can make a big difference. My laptop is a priority. I'd also recommend a clear pencil case to immediately see the things you need, rather than blind rummaging. Schools can support, providing rest breaks when concentration wanes, extra time for class activities and homework hand-ins, and printouts to save copying from the board.

HYPERMOBILITY

Being hypermobile means we're **really** flexible. While manipulating joints out of their expected range is great for contortionists and making people squeamish at parties (guilty!), day to day, it's tedious.

I have frequent neck pain, my muscles and joints ache and my knees click on crouching. I was diagnosed with flat feet at 11. The physiotherapist prescribed customized insoles and 'sensible' shoes to adjust my gait. These, plus train-track braces, NHS glasses and an ill-advised haircut, left me looking like Velma from *Scooby Doo*. Just less attractive.

Again, touch-typing was a saviour here. School can support with rest breaks, allowing us to change position and ease posture. Advance planning for school trips helps limit the physical and emotional toll of trekking around.

GASTROINTESTINAL ISSUES

Or as I call it, dodgy guts. Whether it's chronic constipation, explosive diarrhoea, reflux or agonizing abdominal pain, autism makes us prime sufferers. This causes stress at school.

Canteen dinners of greasy chips and baked beans cause bloating and nausea, so a packed lunch gives you more say over stomach-friendly alternatives. A seat near the classroom door allows for a quick and discreet emergency exit, particularly if you have a 'toilet pass'.

Keep track of your period, too. A sluggish bowel causes constipation pre-period, followed by diarrhoea once you bleed. Tracking my cycle reminds me to make soothing dietary tweaks and prepare for the worse.

DYSLEXIA

While I'm not dyslexic, this learning difficulty is commonly associated with autism. If you have a mare reading, writing and spelling 'correctly', dyslexia may be the culprit.

These signs could sound familiar:

★ Reading and writing slowly.

★ Confusing the order of letters in words, regularly writing them the wrong way round (such as 'b' rather than 'd'); spelling errors are the norm for you.

★ Reading, re-reading, and then reading again, just to get the point of a passage.

★ Understanding information when told verbally, but struggling when it's written down.

★ Trouble planning, organizing and expressing yourself in writing.

Please speak to school. By making adjustments – not asking you to speak aloud in class or penalizing you for incorrect spellings – they can limit your stress and maximize your progress. Getting concise printouts of lesson plans, class notes and homework also reduces the risk of wrongly copying things from the board.

CHAPTER 7

Mental health matters

Autism isn't a mental health problem. It's a developmental condition, affecting how we see the world and interact with people. Having said that, compared to PNTs, we're more prone to mental health issues.

Seven out of ten of us experience challenges, such as anxiety, depression and obsessive compulsive disorder (OCD). What's more, many services tend to focus treatment on either our autism, or our mental health issues, failing to understand the complex connection between the two.

I was diagnosed with clinical depression and anxiety before autism. Anxiety has always played a lead role in the story of my life. My parents still joke that, after three days of labour and me being 12 days overdue, I was too anxious to be born. They're not wrong.

The world is a scary place, particularly because it's built for PNTs. Admittedly, being autistic doesn't guarantee you'll be a bundle of nerves, but according to Dr Luke Beardon in *Autism and Asperger Syndrome in Children*, the golden equation – **autism + environment = outcome** – highlights how our surroundings can up our fret factor.

If our environment feels dodgy, the outcome is anxiety. Luke points out that it's almost impossible for us to learn when we're on high alert. If our teachers and parents can help us identify triggers, we can do our best to manage or eliminate them. This early intervention limits huge problems later in life.

ANXIETY TRIGGERS

■ Stepping into social environments, such as school, and grafting to imitate interactions and edit responses while not necessarily 'getting' what it all means. All this, to fit in and swerve rejection!

- Sensory sensitivities. These build up and overwhelm us as the day goes on.

- Planning and organizing activities, as well as fearing future ones.

- Past triggers, like friendship fallouts or scary settings that caused maximum stress.

- The unpredictable, such as sudden changes, or other people's expectations.

As someone who wears their heart on their sleeve, it's easy to spot when I'm anxious. My mouth runs away with me, as I manically vocalize to anyone who'll listen my emotional torment (upset, anger, frustration, terror) and physical distress (nausea, stomach ache, tight chest, pounding head, etc.).

All this while repeating, 'Is everything going to be okay? Is everything going to be okay?' I **never** go to bed without asking my mum this. I regularly locked myself in the school toilet to panic-text her the same question. Once I'd tearfully given up my location, she texted my key worker to get me out of there.

Having read Naomi Fisher's book *A Different Way to Learn*, I now know that I was fighting to stay inside what neuropsychiatrist Dr Dan Siegel calls the 'window of tolerance' in *The Developing Mind*. This is our personal best state of arousal, one in which we are able to thrive and function.

Sadly, for many, school does not facilitate this best state. Constant demands to tow the PNT line create a toxic environment which, as Naomi describes, leaves us highly prone to anxiety.

Signs include:

★ An extreme need to control situations, such as demanding routines and remaining rigid with requests.

★ Pursuing perfection and becoming angry, upset and frustrated when things fall short.

★ Increased issues with getting to sleep and staying asleep.

★ Becoming paranoid, fixated on one subject, and constantly fearing the worst outcome.

★ Avoiding social situations – including avoiding going to school.

★ Stimming.

★ Self-harm.

★ Meltdowns and shutdowns.

MORE ABOUT SIGNS OF ANXIETY

AVOIDING SOCIAL SITUATIONS

This can be temporary, or permanent. According to Naomi Fisher in *A Different Way to Learn*, many families of neurodivergent children are now swapping standard education systems for self-directed learning.

STIMMING

These are the self-stimulating and repetitive actions we use to help soothe the distress we're feeling. I tend to tap my teeth or forehead or flap my foot at a ridiculous speed. I've also been known to break into a little 'dance', seeking a rhythm to calm myself. It's a hard one for others to get their heads round, so I try to keep it for the privacy of my own home.

Stimming also encompasses our insistence on routines, rituals and intense interests. While my broad ones are currently music, movies and fashion, comedian and author of *Strong Female Character* Fern Brady reminisces how her particular fascination would be whoever she was dating.

SELF-HARM

This is such an emotive (and sometimes triggering) topic for those who harm and those who care about us, but I can't pretend it doesn't happen. Being autistic makes us more prone to self-harm as we become emotionally overwhelmed and can't find the words to express it.

Harming is a coping mechanism. It takes many forms, like scratching, picking, burning and hitting ourselves. Episodes of alcohol or drug misuse, or over-

or under-eating, may be deliberate acts of self-harm, as well as risky sexual behaviour.

There's not necessarily one motive. I've heard many reasons, including diverting emotional pain like anger into physical pain because it causes 'real' feelings. It also arouses sensation, breaking feelings of numbness.

Personally, I've punished myself for not feeling good enough, particularly when it comes to peer relations. I've rationalized (wrongly) that it's something I deserve. I've told myself that something 'even worse' will happen if I don't do it.

I know it's hard resisting the urge to harm. It can feel like the only way of coping when you're emotionally dysregulated. But any brief moment of relief I feel is replaced by deeper sadness, particularly when I see how hard it is for my parents to understand.

My dad can't get his head around why I'll stress over spots but 'willingly' scar my skin. Logically, it doesn't make sense. But our emotional mind pushes the wise one offline when we're overwhelmed. That's why some self-compassion is critical.

Please don't beat yourself up on top of everything else. Instead, try to recognize your triggers (mine tends to be friendship difficulties), and find ways of distracting from or delaying urges.

Different distractions work for different people, and the same might not work every time. If you're raging, pummelling your pillow or going for a run might help. If you're sad, cocooning yourself in a blanket or hugging your pet could work.

I always have an ice pack in the freezer to shock me out of a furious state, and find standing under a hot shower is soothing. My dog is also no stranger to my tears. Please go gently and know that there is always support (go to the FYI section at the end of the book and look up Self-Injury Support, the National Self Harm Network and the Calm Harm app).

MELTDoWNS AND SHUTDoWNS

While both are a clear sign that we've reached crisis point and can't cope with school, meltdowns and shutdowns look and feel different.

Meltdowns. Meltdowns are explosive, an outward display of the anxiety we've accumulated over the last hours, days or weeks. I'm like a volcano, erupting, my swear-fuelled lava scorching everything in its path. The lack of control I feel is hideous, as are the resulting tears and shame.

Then there's the physical damage. I fashioned my own fringe as a child after pulling out my hair. I still have a lopsided drawer in my bedroom where I kicked it off its runners.

Many times, I've been labelled a drama queen, accused of throwing toddler-style tantrums. Dr Luke Beardon says this is an unfair and inaccurate comparison to make, while Fern Brady brands it absurd in *Strong Female Character*. Tantrums suggest control or manipulation, that we're deliberately going off on one to get our needs met.

Meltdowns are nothing of the sort. They're reactions to extreme stress and must be acknowledged as such. Clearly, arsey behaviour isn't easy for our teachers or parents (or friends) to let go. But reprimanding us doesn't work. It's punitive and unfair when we have no control.

THE AUTISTIC TEEN GIRL'S SCHOOL SURVIVAL GUIDE

Shutdowns. Although meltdowns are hard to miss, shutdowns are more subtle. It's a bit like being a car with no petrol. The bodywork looks intact, but there's no fuel to start the engine.

Our ability to process what's going on is severely hindered; we can become mute or frozen, unable to even move from a classroom, for example. When I shutdown, I feel hollow. My whole body aches. The most I can do is lie in bed and stare at the walls.

These aren't dreamy duvet days. They're the nightmarish numbness that comes from school burnout. I've experienced episodes lasting from hours to days. It's totally crap for me, but it's probably worse for my parents seeing me so low. They say I'm 'unreachable', and they've learned not to try.

Things that help. Pooling our learned wisdom, my parents and I have found the following can help:

★ Keep calm. Meltdowns are scary to witness but don't tell us to stop or snap out of it. Limit questions. Just let us know you're there for us.

★ Shutdowns act like a reset. Give us time and

space to rest and recover without making demands.

★ Talk to us when we're not stressed to find out what helps when we're melting or shutting down. Georgia Harper, autistic campaigner and Policy and Public Affairs Officer for national research charity Autistica, suggests using calm moments to identify patterns and triggers, be they sensory overload or changes in routine.

★ Use energy accounting to avoid going overdrawn.

ENERGY ACCOUNTING

Energy accounting involves working out what saps and boosts your energy. Imagine your resources, like a bank account or battery. Throughout the day you'll do stuff that withdraws energy, regular activities, like getting ready for school, or occasional events, like going to a party.

Then there's the stuff that recharges your battery or puts a deposit in your account, like listening to music or indulging special interests. The model, devised by

Maja Toudal and co-created with Dr Tony Attwood, recommends making a list of things that drain and boost your battery, rating each out of 10.

For example:

Energy drainers	Energy boosters
Dentist visit (−7)	Listening to music (+8)
Speaking in class (−9)	Going for a walk (+7)
Going to a party (−8)	Having a hot chocolate (+5)
Sitting exams (−10)	Deep breathing (+6)

When several withdrawals are made, deposits need topping up, preventing us going overdrawn and triggering a meltdown or shutdown. If you know visiting the dentist will sap your energy, you can boost your balance by going for a walk or listening to music.

It's essential for self-care, particularly after a tough day at school. I typically took an hour to decompress once home, soaking away the stress with a hot bath, then watching Netflix and cuddling my dog. It helped me recharge and be more able to face homework.

PROFESSIONAL HELP

Self-help is a great starting point, but sometimes outside support is needed, particularly if you're using coping mechanisms like self-harm to manage, or your mood is consistently low, leaving you feeling suicidal. Talking to someone you trust, like a friend, parent, teacher or pastoral support, or using external resources, like websites and helplines are effective steps towards getting help (go to the FYI section at the end of the book, and look up Childline, Kooth, Papyrus and Shout).

Your GP might refer you to CAMHS (Child and Adolescent Mental Health Services) or provide details for other mental health agencies offering counselling. Sure, it's a bit weird at first sharing your inner turmoil with a stranger but, as Mair Elliott points out, recognizing and expressing your emotions is healthier than holding them in.

I'm a complete fan of counselling. I've been seeing my

therapist, Julie, for six years. I will be priority guest-listing her for my wedding. (No, no proposal as yet!)

CHAPTER 8

Life beyond school

Honestly, I never thought I'd see the back of school. Yet, here I am. Admittedly, I'm still in education, but with a great deal more freedom and self-directed learning at university.

What's more, rather than restricted by compulsory school subjects, I'm playing to my strengths and doing a Drama degree. My strong memory helps with learning lines, and following a script means I don't have to worry about what to say next — it's all written down for me. Years of masking have primed me in pretending to be someone else, too!

While this is my choice, yours may be taking an apprenticeship. This lets you study, work and earn some cash, all at once. Or perhaps you want to go straight into getting a job. Talk to your teachers and career advisors for appropriate next steps. The National Careers Service has great advice on suitable work opportunities or training, too (go to the FYI section at the end of the book).

If you're passionate about continuing your studies, the University and Colleges Admission website holds a wealth of information on courses and colleges and how to apply (go to the FYI section at the end of the book). I found their staff incredibly helpful, not batting an eyelid when, last minute, I chose to protect my mental health, swapping my destination from three hours to 90 minutes from home.

Location, and other factors, are really worth considering:

★ Location. Would you be happier living away from home or studying locally? If you relocate, are there decent and affordable transport links so you can head home for regular respite?

★ Environment. Remember Dr Luke Beardon's golden equation from Chapter 7? Environment has a huge impact on our anxiety levels, so suss out your sensory needs in terms of accommodation, eating, entertainment venues, lecture rooms, etc.

★ Social opportunities. Meeting people and making friends feels overwhelming when you're new to campus. Joining clubs and societies that feed your special interests provides structured socializing with like-minded types.

★ Support. Universities and colleges are tooled up for supporting students with additional needs. My academic tutors, personal advisor and staff at the wellbeing hub have all steadied my transition. Before making your final choice, do quiz colleges on their understanding of autism and co-occurring challenges, and what learning and wellbeing provisions are available. Get advice on all available funding, too, including the Disabled Students' Allowance (DSA) (go to the FYI section at the end of the book).

Whichever route you choose, know that our drive for perfection, attention to detail, amazing memories and exceptional honesty make us hugely employable. Do not let your diagnosis stand in your way. In fact, follow Jo Egerton's advice, searching out strong female autistic role models who have made the world a better place.

Here's some inspirational autistic and/or ADHD women to start you off:

- ★ Courtney Love, musician

- ★ Sia, singer

- ★ Greta Thunberg, climate activist

- ★ Daryl Hannah, Hollywood actress

- ★ Fern Brady, comedian and author

- ★ Melanie Sykes, TV presenter

- ★ Temple Grandin, scientist, author and autism advocate

- ★ Christine McGuiness, model, author and reality TV star

- ★ Jessica-Jane Applegate MBE, paralympic swimmer

- ★ Greta Gerwig, actor, writer and director

- ★ Emma Watson, actor and feminist campaigner

★ Simone Biles, Olympic and world gold medallist gymnast

★ Paris Hilton, heiress, socialite and entrepreneur

★ Margot Robbie, actress

★ Raven Baxter, molecular biologist and science communicator

★ Lily Allen, singer and actress

★ Sue Perkins, comedian and writer

★ Cara Delevingne, model, actor and musician

★ Mel B, singer and Spice Girl!

CHAPTER 9

Looking forward

Opening my laptop and tapping out this journey has been a gruelling but cathartic experience.

To begin, I was really reluctant 'going public' with my diagnosis. I feared judgment, being misunderstood or bullied. But reading up on neurodiversity and talking to experts and fellow autistic supergirls has revealed the benefits of 'coming out'.

In *Spectrum Women*, author Barb Cook describes the sense of relief perfectly. It's like taking off a corset (or a mask!) you didn't even know you were wearing. Finally, you're able to breathe.

Seriously, pretending to be someone else is suffocating. I'm therefore working hard to celebrate the real me. I've elected not to limit myself or be limited by others, embracing my authentic self in true 'you do you' fashion.

I wish the same for you. Which is why I wrote this book. I know it's a cliché, but if I knew then what I know now, my school experience may have been less brutal.

Perhaps with the right support, from the right people...

> Concrete teaching techniques adapted to meet the demands of my neurodiverse brain, delivered by understanding, accepting and empathic teachers...

...I would have felt more able to learn.

Perhaps with a kinder environment...

> Simple classroom adjustments to soothe rather than savage my sensory sensitivities, and positive peer relations encouraged through structured and monitored clubs...

...my self-esteem would have been greater and burnout less.

Perhaps then, with higher confidence and more motivation...

> Committing to self-care through energy accounting, or colour coding my learning materials to ease my wonky executive functioning...

...I could have managed greater personal responsibility, too.

Perhaps...

...Perhaps...

...Perhaps.

I could drive myself mad with 'what ifs'. But I've spent too much time feeling outraged at the standard education system, distressed at being different, guilty for not fitting in. It's a waste of negative energy, energy I'd rather spend on educating the educators and encouraging true inclusivity.

I also know that I have much to be grateful for – like a family who have never given up on me, and a trusted key worker who tirelessly supported my final years through school. During times of high stress and burnout, she tweaked my timetable, allowing mental health days at home.

Because that's the thing. Sometimes, we just can't go to school. That meant days and weeks off for me. For you, it might be more permanent.

Honestly, nothing is worth making yourself continually physically and mentally ill over. If the standard education system is causing untold agony to you and your family, **please** consider the alternatives. As Naomi Fisher points out in *A Different Way to Learn*, self-directed education can help neurodiverse young people develop at their own pace and thrive.

Ultimately, whether you decide to learn at home, or choose to stick with school, I hope the challenging encounters I've shared help make yours brighter. Yes, being autistic will influence our experiences. But it doesn't have to dictate them.

Remember, you do you!

Wishing you well.
Gracie x

FYI

AUTISM

Ambitious about Autism is a national charity for children and young people, raising awareness and understanding around autism: www.ambitiousaboutautism.org.uk

Autistica is the UK's leading autism research and campaigning charity: www.autistica.org.uk

The Curly Hair Project was founded by author and campaigner Alis Rowe, and provides support, as well as information and training opportunities around autism: www.thegirlwiththecurlyhair.co.uk

Mair Elliott, a young patient activist, offers honest and open talk about day-to-day living with mental health challenges and autism: https://mairelliott97.wixsite.com/mysite

The National Autistic Society provides support and information on autism for individuals: www.autism.org.uk

Quantum Leap Mentoring, a website from Siena Castellon, autism advocate and author of *The Spectrum Girl's Survival Guide*, provides child-friendly information on autism, dyspraxia and dyslexia, and tips on how to succeed at school: https://neurodiversity.wixsite.com/qlmentoring

MENTAL HEALTH AND WELLBEING

Alumina is a free, online seven-week course for young people struggling with self-harm. Each group is made up of 14 people, aged 10–17, sharing non-judgemental space to explore emotions and self-help strategies: www.selfharm.co.uk

Anti-Bullying Alliance is a coalition of organizations and individuals united against bullying, providing help for those impacted:

www.anti-bullyingalliance.org.uk (for a definition
of bullying, see https://anti-bullyingalliance.org.uk/
tools-information/all-about-bullying/understanding-
bullying/definition)

Bullying UK (Family Lives) offers advice around all
aspects of bullying, including physical, emotional,
online and at school: www.familylives.org.uk

Calm Harm is an app providing distraction
techniques and tools to help you regulate your
thoughts and feelings, managing the urge to self-
harm: https://calmharm.stem4.org.uk

Childline offers confidential support around
bullying, family conflict, sex and relationships,
as well as school pressures. Text or call 0800 1111:
www.childline.org.uk

Kooth is an online counselling and wellbeing hub for
children and young people: www.kooth.com

National Self Harm Network (NSHN) is a national
forum supporting individuals who self-harm to reduce
emotional distress and improve their quality of life:
www.nshn.co.uk

Papyrus is a national charity dedicated to the prevention of young suicide. Confidential support is available on HOPELINE247 0800 068 41 41: www.papyrus-uk.org

Self-Injury Support, in addition to online self-help resources, offers confidential support from 7pm–10pm, every Monday and Thursday by phone 0808 800 8088 or text 07537 432 44: www.selfinjurysupport.org.uk

Shout provides tools to manage your mental health, while online counsellors can be confidentially contacted, 24/7, by texting 'shout' to 85258: www.giveusashout.org

YoungMinds is the UK's leading charity for children and young people's mental health providing information around diagnoses and support: www.youngminds.org.uk

ADDITIONAL DIAGNOSES

ADHD Foundation Neurodiversity Charity is an integrated health and education service offering specific advice to young people with ADHD: www.adhdfoundation.org.uk

The British Dyslexia Association is a membership organization working to achieve a dyslexia-friendly society for all: www.bdadyslexia.org.uk

The Dyslexia Association provides a breadth of expert advice to improve the lives of dyslexics of all ages as well as support for families, educators and employers: www.dyslexia.uk.net

GOVERNMENT ADVICE

Disabled Students' Allowance provides help if you're a student with a learning difficulty, health problem or disability: www.gov.uk/disabled-students-allowance-dsa

National Careers Service provides careers information, advice and guidance, at all stages in your career: https://nationalcareers.service.gov.uk

Universities and Colleges Admissions Service (UCAS) helps you explore your options to make the next step in higher education: www.ucas.com

GOOD BOOKS

A Different Way to Learn: Neurodiversity and Self-Directed Education by Naomi Fisher (Jessica Kingsley Publishers, 2023)

Asperger's and Girls by Tony Attwood and Temple Grandin (Future Horizons, 2016)

Aspergirls: Empowering Females with Asperger Syndrome by Rudy Simone (Jessica Kingsley Publishers, 2010)

Autism and Asperger Syndrome in Children: For Parents of the Newly Diagnosed by Luke Beardon (Sheldon Press, 2019)

Can't Not Won't: A Story about a Child Who Couldn't Go to School by Eliza Fricker (Jessica Kingsley Publishers, 2023)

Dyslexia is My Superpower (Most of the Time) by Margaret Rooke (Jessica Kingsley Publishers, 2017)

Educating and Supporting Autistic Girls: A Resource for Mainstream Education and Health Professionals by Victoria Honeybourne (Routledge, 2023)

Energy Accounting: Stress Management and Mental Health Monitoring for Autism and Related Conditions by Maja Toudal and Dr Anthony Attwood (Jessica Kingsley Publishers, 2024)

From Hurt to Hope: Stories of Mental Health, Mental Illness, and Being Autistic by Mair Elliott (Jessica Kingsley Publishers, 2021)

Girls and Autism: Educational, Family and Personal Perspectives edited by Barry Carpenter, Francesca Happé and Jo Egerton (Routledge, 2019)

M is for Autism by The Students of Limpsfield Grange School and Vicky Martin (Jessica Kingsley Publishers, 2015)

Spectrum Women: Walking to the Beat of Autism edited by Barb Cook and Michelle Garnett (Jessica Kingsley Publishers, 2018)

Strong Female Character by Fern Brady (Brazen, 2023)

The Developing Mind: How Relationships and the Brain Interact to Shape Who We Are by Daniel Siegel (Guilford Press, 2020)

The Girl with the Curly Hair: Asperger's and Me by Alis Rowe (Lonely Mind Books, 2013)

The Spectrum Girl's Survival Guide: How to Grow Up Awesome and Autistic by Siena Castellon (Jessica Kingsley Publishers, 2020)

The Teenage Girl's Guide to Living Well with ADHD: Improve Your Self-Esteem, Self-Care and Self Knowledge by Sonia Ali (Jessica Kingsley Publishers, 2021)

Understanding ADHD in Girls and Women edited by Joanne Steer (Jessica Kingsley Publishers, 2021)

Index